twilight
the score

ISBN 978-1-4234-6906-3

HAL•LEONARD®
CORPORATION
7777 W. BLUEMOUND RD. P.O. BOX 13819 MILWAUKEE, WI 53213

In Australia Contact:
Hal Leonard Australia Pty. Ltd.
4 Lentara Court
Cheltenham, Victoria, 3192 Australia
Email: ausadmin@halleonard.com.au

Visit Hal Leonard Online at
www.halleonard.com

WHO ARE THEY?

Composed by CARTER BURWELL

Moderately fast

mp

Pedal ad lib. throughout

4

(Pedal simile throughout)

6

Slightly slower

PHASCINATION PHASE

Composed by CARTER BURWELL

Moderately slow, in 2

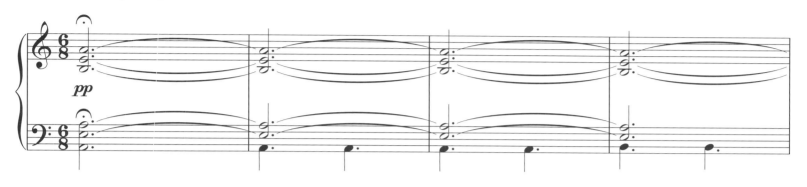

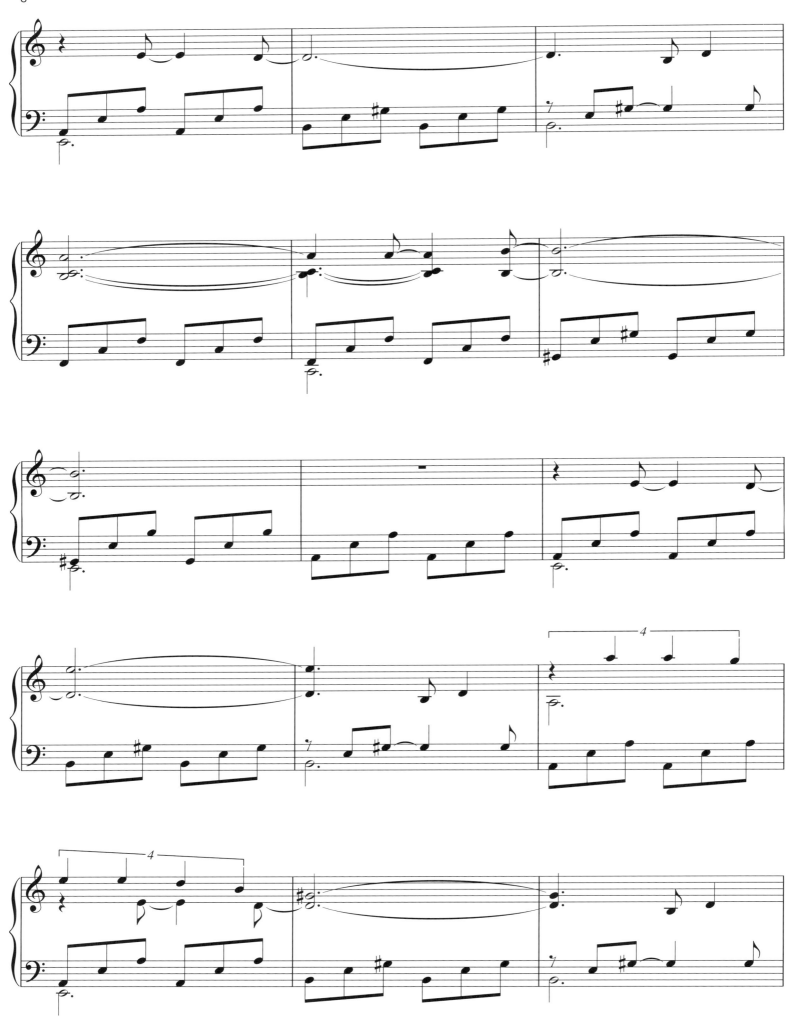

I DREAMT OF EDWARD

Composed by CARTER BURWELL

THE LION FELL IN LOVE WITH THE LAMB

Composed by CARTER BURWELL

Moderately slow, in 2

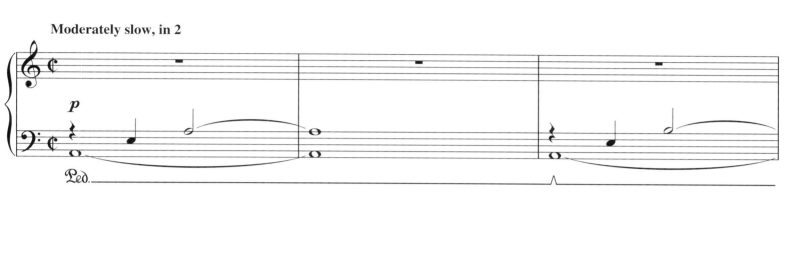

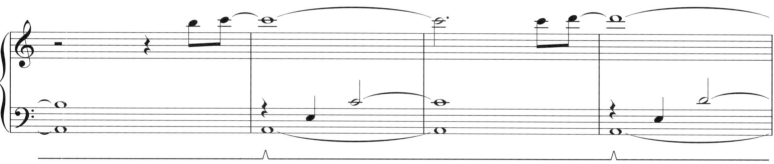

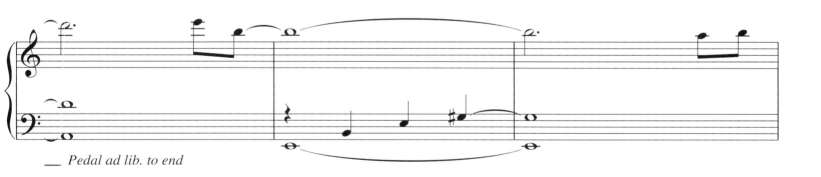

Pedal ad lib. to end

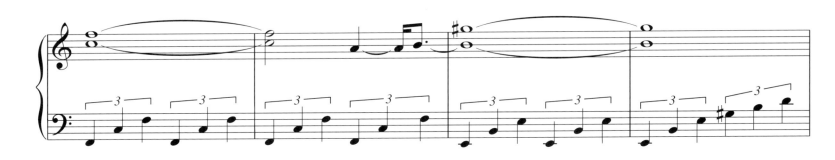

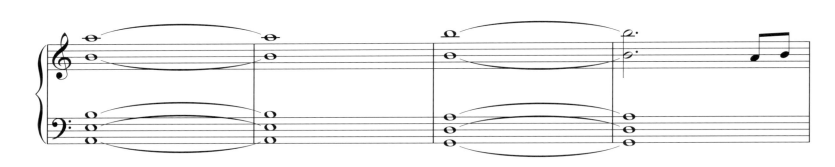

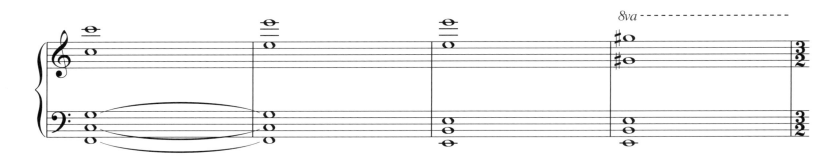

DINNER WITH HIS FAMILY

Composed by CARTER BURWELL

BELLA'S LULLABY

Composed by CARTER BURWELL
(for Christine)

I WOULD BE THE MEAL

Composed by CARTER BURWELL

STUCK HERE LIKE MOM

Composed by CARTER BURWELL

TRACKING

Composed by CARTER BURWELL

Slowly, in 2

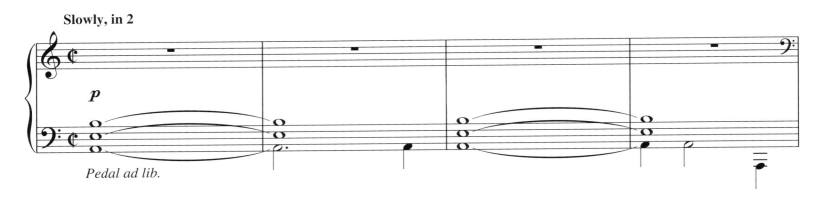

Pedal ad lib.

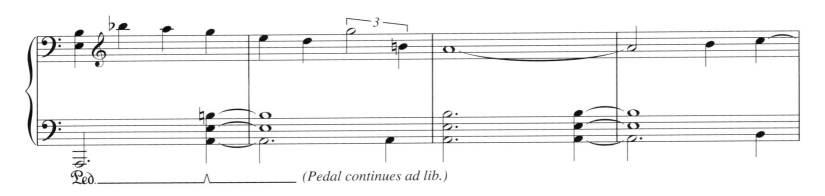

Ped._____ (Pedal continues ad lib.)

IN PLACE OF SOMEONE YOU LOVE

Composed by CARTER BURWELL

Moderately

Pedal ad lib. throughout

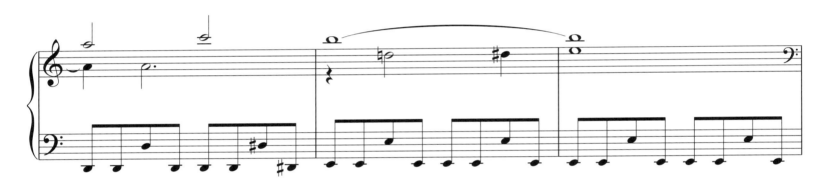

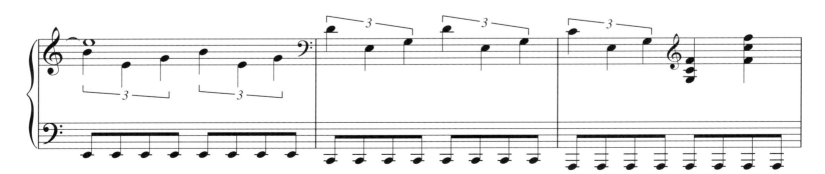

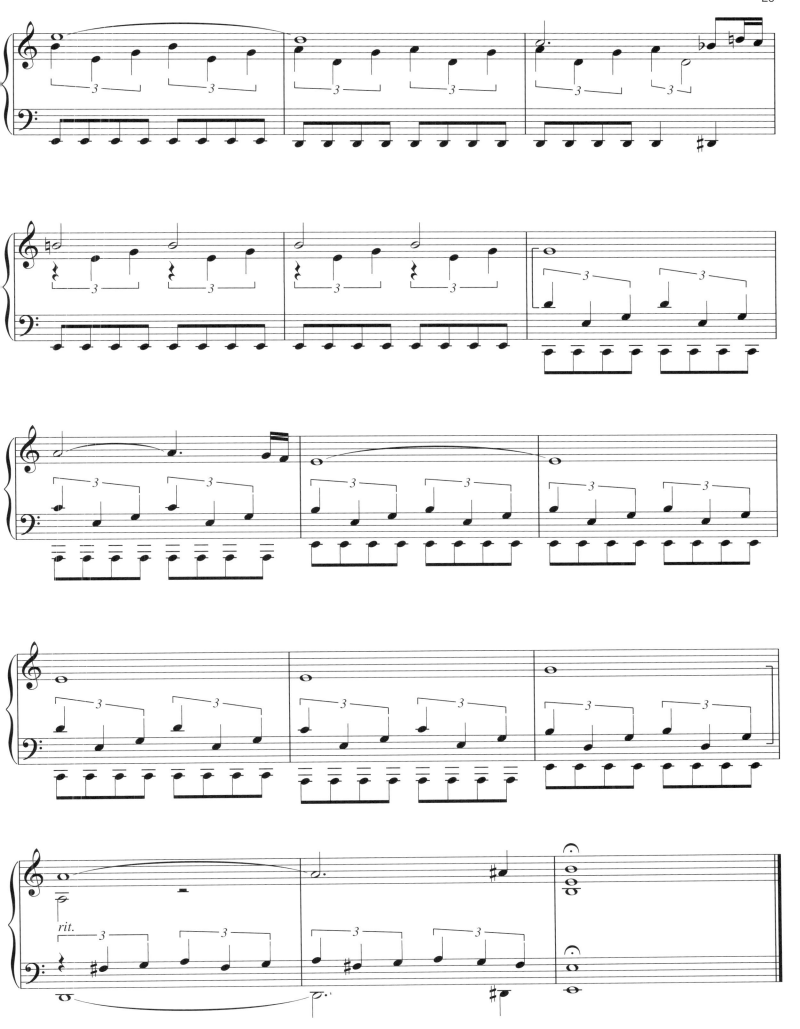

EDWARD AT HER BED

Composed by CARTER BURWELL